D0917924

# FAITHFUL TO THE END

*Also by Celia Haddon*

A CHRISTMAS POSY

A LOVER'S POSY

A MOTHER'S POSY

A BOOK OF FRIENDS AND FRIENDSHIP

THE YEARBOOK OF HOPE AND INSPIRATION

THE YEARBOOK OF COMFORT AND JOY

THE YEARBOOK OF COURAGE AND SERENITY

THE LOVE OF CATS:
*THE DAILY TELEGRAPH* ANTHOLOGY OF CATS

MISCHIEF AND DELIGHT:
AN ILLUSTRATED ANTHOLOGY OF KITTENS (*with Jess McAree)*

# FAITHFUL TO THE END

## An Illustrated
## Anthology of Dogs

## CELIA HADDON

HEADLINE

Copyright © 1991 Celia Haddon

The right of Celia Haddon to be identified as the
author of the Work has been asserted by her in accordance
with the Copyright, Designs and Patents Act 1988.

First published in 1991
by HEADLINE BOOK PUBLISHING PLC

First published in paperback in 1993
by HEADLINE BOOK PUBLISHING PLC

10 9 8 7 6 5 4 3 2 1

All rights reserved. No part of this publication may be
reproduced, stored in a retrieval system, or transmitted,
in any form or by any means without the prior written
permission of the publisher, nor be otherwise circulated
in any form of binding or cover other than that in which
it is published and without a similar condition being
imposed on the subsequent purchaser.

ISBN 0 7472 4348 4

Design and computer page make up by Penny Mills

Printed and bound in Great Britain by
Butler & Tanner Ltd, Frome and London

HEADLINE BOOK PUBLISHING PLC
Headline House
79 Great Titchfield Street
London W1P 7FN

## To Merlin

## To a Dog

With eye upraised his master's look to scan,
The joy, the solace, and the aid of man;
The rich man's guardian and the poor man's friend,
The only creature faithful to the end.

ANONYMOUS

# Author's Note

Please remember lost, abandoned and abused dogs by
supporting dog rescue societies like
the National Canine Defence League,
1 Pratt Street, London NW1.

# CONTENTS

# THE BEST OF FRIENDS

A loving friendship, formed over thousands of years, flourishes between dogs and human beings. Dogs have left the hunting pack of their ancestors and have become members of our human world. They are our uncomplaining servants, our playful companions, and loving members of our families.

How strange it is that two quite different species should become so close to each other. We belong to different families on the evolutionary tree. They have four feet and fur. We have two and none. We have completely different ways of communicating. Dogs cannot speak our complicated verbal language nor can we communicate in their equally subtle language of smell.

Yet we love each other. We understand and empathise across this great gulf. Man and dog (or woman and dog) have often been closer than man and wife. And, stranger still, we take all this for granted.

Sociologists have dissected the modern family. Anthropologists have examined primitive human societies. Zoologists have carefully documented the behaviour of wild animals. Yet the furry friend with the melting eyes that lives in our home was till recently ignored by all of them. Only in the last few years has anybody started researching the relationship between man and dog.

This age-old friendship is threatened by people who want to tidy up the world. In the past dictators and tyrannical regimes have forbidden dog shows and sometimes even slaughtered pet dogs in the name of efficiency. Today bureaucrats have banned dogs from parks, from beaches, from shops and from places of entertainment – in the name of hygiene. Intellectuals have sneered at the human-dog friendship and condemned it as 'sentimental'. Yet, despite their hostile propaganda, the loving bond between our two species persists. Neither tyrants nor bureaucrats nor intellectual snobs can abolish this love, thank goodness. For though we talk of a man and 'his' dog, the relationship is a surprisingly equal one. Human history bears witness to the way 'owners' have loved their dogs and have felt that a dog often is their best friend. Even kings have been devoted to dogs. Charles II, the dashing Stuart king of Britain, had a train of little spaniels that followed him everywhere, going out for walks with him, sitting at his feet during Privy Council meetings and even having their puppies in his bedroom. In modern times a little pack of corgis and corgi crossbreds lives with Queen Elizabeth II in Buckingham Palace, and across the Atlantic several dogs have lived at the White House in Washington DC.

Some of the greatest writers in the English language have loved dogs. The poet Alexander Pope, in a letter describing his dog, summed up the relationship this way: 'If it be the chief point of friendship to comply with a friend's motions and inclinations, he possesses this in an eminent degree; he lies down when I sit, and walks when I walk, which is more than many good friends can pretend to.'

We dog-lovers are in the best company, as the poems and letters in this chapter prove. We need not feel embarrassed by our devotion to dogs. This book celebrates an enduring friendship.

All real dog-lovers talk to their dogs. Sir Walter Scott, a great dog-lover, was no exception. Washington Irving, the American essayist, described a visit to the great Scottish novelist in 1817. They went for a walk, taking the dogs with them, naturally.

> As we sallied forth, every dog in the establishment turned out to attend us. There was the old staghound, Maida, a noble animal; and Hamlet, the black greyhound, a wild, thoughtless youngster, not yet arrived at the years of discretion; and Finette, a beautiful setter, with soft, silken hair, long pendant ears, and a mild eye, the parlour favourite. When in front of the house, we were joined by a superannuated greyhound, who came from the kitchen wagging his tail; and was cheered by Scott as an old friend and comrade. In our walks, he would frequently pause in conversation, to notice his dogs, and speak to them as if rational companions; and indeed there appears to be a vast deal of rationality in these faithful attendants on man, derived from their close intimacy with him... His domestic animals were his friends...

One of the greatest dog-lovers was Elizabeth Barrett Browning, the Victorian poet who married Robert Browning. She was given a spaniel by her friend Mary Russell Mitford, which she named Flush. She spoiled him shamelessly, as her letters to her friend make clear.

*4 November 1842*
I think more and more of him. You will admit him to be improved as to ears & pretty curling hair, but *spiritually* he grows dearer & dearer. He will sleep at nights, now, no where except with his head on my shoulder... If you were but to see him eat partridge from a silver fork... Of course, he has given up his ice creams for the season, – and the favourite substitute seems to be coffee – and coffee, understand, not poured into the saucer, but taken out of my little coffee cup... he sees that I drink out of the cup and not out of the saucer; and in spite of his nose, he will do the same. My dear pretty little Flushie!

*21 November 1842*
My Flush clearly understands articulate language – only I think, at least I have thought, that it is rather particular words & phrases, which he understands, than the construction & modification of language. 'Dinner', 'cakes', 'milk', 'go downstairs', 'go out', everybody's name in the house, 'go & kiss Miss Barrett', 'kiss' (abstractedly) – 'kiss the hand', 'kiss the face' – my Flush understands and applies all that as well as Dr Johnson could have done.

*6 August 1844*
Here is Flush, rejoicing like Bacchus himself, among the grapes! eating one grape after another, with exceeding complacency, shown by swingings of the tail. 'Very good grapes, indeed!'

Naturally she wrote poems about Flush. She described one incident in her letters to Mrs Mitford, and then wrote a poem about it. Here is her account first in prose then in poetry.

*2 October 1843*
I, who had had my heart full for hours, took advantage of an early moment of solitude, to cry in it very bitterly. Suddenly a little hairy head thrust itself from behind my pillow into my face, rubbing its ears & nose against me in a responsive agitation, & drying the tears as they came. I had forgotten Flushie, and was startled at the apparition, or rather the sensation, of the hairy head – it was a Faunus or a Pan!

## Flush or Faunus

You see this dog? It was but yesterday
I mused forgetful of his presence here,
Till thought on thought drew downward tear on tear,
When from the pillow, where wet-cheeked I lay,
A head, as hairy as Faunus, thrust its way
Right sudden against my face, – two golden-clear
Great eyes astonished mine, – a drooping ear
Did flap me on either cheek to dry the spray!
I started first, as some Arcadian,
Amazed by goatly god in twilight grove;
But, as the bearded vision closelier ran
My tears off, I knew Flush, and rose above
Surprise and sadness, – thanking the true Pan,
Who, by low creatures, leads to heights of love.

[13]

Henry James, the American novelist, wrote to Louisa Horstmann in 1904, when he was about to let her his house in Rye, Sussex. After telling her about his servant, he asked her to look after Max, his dachshund.

I take the liberty of confiding to your charity and humanity the precious little person of my dachshund Max, who is the best and gentlest and most reasonable and well-mannered, as well as the most beautiful small animal of his kind to be easily come across – so that I think you will speedily find yourselves loving him for his own sweet sake. The servants, who are very fond of him and good to him, know what he 'has', and when he has it; and I shall take it kindly if he be not too often gratified with tidbits between meals. Of course what he most intensely dreams of is being taken out on walks, and the more you are able to indulge him the more he will adore you and the more all the latent beauty of his nature will come out. He is, I am happy to say, and has been from the first (he is about a year and a half old) in very good, plain, straightforward health, and if he is not overfed, and is sufficiently exercised, and adequately brushed (his brush being always in one of the bowls on the hall-table – a convenient little currycomb) and Burgess is allowed occasionally to wash him, I have no doubt he will remain very fit.

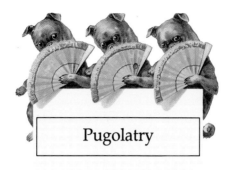

## Pugolatry

Within the centre of a rose
My eye, in fancy, doth impose
The dear crinkles of thy face –
Ah yes! in truth in *ev'ry* place:
Within a blanket's crumpled fold
Thy furrowed brow I do behold,
And even o'er a dish of tea
The teapot speaks to me of thee
And sugar tongs thy legs suggest.
Sweet pug, my eyes now never rest
On anything or anywhere
But thou imaginéd art there.
The whorléd temple of the snail?
Fern's crozier'd tip? Thy curly tail!
Owls, agile spiders, otters, seals,
Frogs, bumblebees – each swift reveals
A pug to my enslavéd soul.
Throughout this world from pole to pole
All that can walk or fly or swim
Finds part of thee in part of them.
*Thus, though thy life may little be,*
*Love builds thine immortality.*

HARO HODSON

[15]

Dogs have a special place in the lives of those people who are lonely or unhappy. Ebenezer Elliott was a minor poet, an iron merchant who also wrote verses, many of which denounced the social evils of the nineteenth century. But among his poems are these touching lines. I felt they should be included, because they express what so many of us feel in times of great discouragement: it can be our dogs that give us a reason for going on.

## My Only Friends

My heart grows sick when home I come –
My God the thought forgive!
If 'twere not for my cat and dog
I think I could not live.
My cat and dog when I come home
Run out to welcome me;
She, mewing with her tail on end,
While wagging his comes he.
They listen for my homeward steps,
My smothered sob they hear,
When down my heart sinks, deathly down,
Because my home is near…

Why come they not? They do not come
My breaking heart to meet;
A heavier darkness on me falls,
I cannot lift my feet.
Oh, yes, they come – they never fail
To listen for my sighs;
My poor heart brightens when it meets
The sunshine of their eyes.
Again they come to meet me – God!
Wilt thou the thought forgive?
If 'twere not for my cat and dog
I think I could not live...

My playful cat and honest dog
Are all the friends I have.

I have always imagined that the Victorian novelist George Eliot was a rather over-serious and earnest woman. Yet she had her softer side. On 30 July 1859, she wrote to her friend John Blackwood about a pug that he had bought for her. Her letter reveals her delight at her new friend.

Pug is come! – come to fill up the void left by false and narrow-hearted friends. I see already that he is without envy, hatred, or malice – that he will betray no secrets, and feel neither pain at my success nor pleasure in my chagrin. I hope the photograph does justice to his physiognomy. It is expressive, full of gentleness and affection, and radiant with intelligence when there is a savoury morsel in question – a hopeful indication of his mental capacity. I distrust all intellectual pretension that announces itself by obtuseness of palate!

I wish you could see him in his best pose, – when I have arrested him in a violent career of carpet-scratching, and he looks at me with fore-legs very wide apart, trying to penetrate the deep mystery of this arbitrary, not to say capricious, prohibition. He is snoring by my side at this moment, with a serene promise of remaining quiet for any length of time: he couldn't behave better if he had been expressly educated for me.

## An Address to his Auld Dog, Hector

Come, my auld, towzy, trusty friend,
What gars ye look sae dung wi' wae?
D'ye think my favour's at an end,
Because thy head is turnin' gray?

Although thy strength begins to fail,
Its best was spent in serving me;
An' can I grudge thy wee bit meal,
Some comfort in thy age to gie?

For mony a day, frae sun to sun,
We've toiled fu' hard wi' ane anither;
An' mony a thousand mile thou'st run,
To keep my thraward flocks thegither.

I ne'er could thole thy cravin' face,
Nor when ye pattit on my knee;
Though in a far an' unco place,
I've whiles been forced to beg for thee.

I'll get a cottage o' my ain,
Some wee bit cannie, lonely biel',
Where thy auld heart shall rest fu' fain,
An' share wi' me my humble meal.

JAMES HOGG

[19]

Queen Victoria was passionately attached to her dogs. She mentions some of them in her *More Leaves from the Journal of a Life in the Highlands*. 'My favourite collie Noble is always down-stairs when we take our meals, and was so good, Brown making him lie on a chair or couch, and he never attempted to come down without per-mission, and even held a piece of cake in his mouth without eating it, till told he might,' she writes at one point.

During her life she had scores of dogs including collies, a Pekinese, Pomeranians, dachshunds, greyhounds and a rare Tibetan mastiff. She refused to let her dogs be mutilated by having their tails docked and often had their portraits specially painted.

Her first love, however, was her first dog, a spaniel called Dash. She was painted with him in the 1830s, when she was just eleven years old. In her diary are these delightful entries about Dash.

*23 April 1833*
I dressed <u>dear sweet little Dash</u> for the second time after dinner in a scarlet jacket and blue trousers.

*9 January 1839*
I sent for Dashy, who Lord M[elbourne] accused of having crooked legs, which I wouldn't allow! We put him on the table and he was very much petted and admired by Lord M, who was so funny about him! We gave him tea and Lord M said, 'I wonder if lapping is a pleasant sensation,' – for that is a thing we had never felt.

Devotion to dogs is found in surprising places. Colonel George Hanger wrote a book, *To All Sportsmen*, in 1814, in which he reveals that he and Lord Thanet (the father of a friend) had an unexpectedly soft spot for dogs. I felt his words should be in this book, to represent all those tough, sporting men who are so gentle and loving to their dogs.

I always make my dogs my companions in the shooting season; taking them into the room where I sit, after I am returned from the field; letting them bask themselves by the fire, which comforts them, and does them a great deal of good, especially when, after rain, the turnips are very wet. This method, I am certain, prevents many from having the rheumatism. Would you like, when you return from shooting, to be put into a parlour, as they call it, at an ale house, in which there has not been a fire lighted for a week? Lord Thanet, the father of my worthy and kind friend, the present Lord, was a great fox-hunter. He had a kennel so constituted, on purpose for his hounds, with a large circular place in the centre railed off, which contained a very large coal fire; the kennel-man always at night, replenishing the fire. Round this the hounds lay and basked themselves, after the day's chase; by which, I trust it will be allowed, they were materially benefited.

This is my favourite among modern poems about dogs. Stevie Smith, who died in 1971, had a special affection for and empathy with animals. The poem recalls a moment of tenderness for an old dog, for it is dedicated 'to the Brownes' pug dog, on my lap, in their car, coming home from Norfolk'.

This particular pug was called Foss (pedigree name Richard Lionheart). Pugs were originally temple dogs, whose job it was to chase off demons by barking at them. Though a modern dog, Foss took this ancient responsibility very seriously. He used to chase aeroplanes, rushing out into the garden and barking at them till they flew away. Then he would come in again, breathing rather heavily, with an expression of satisfaction at a job well done.

## O Pug!

O Pug, some people do not like you,
But I like you,
Some people say you do not breathe, you snore,
I don't mind,
One person says he is always conscious of your behind,
Is that your fault?

Your own people love you,
All the people in the family that owns you
Love you: Good pug, they cry, Happy pug,
Pug-come-for-a-walk.

You are an old dog now
And in all your life
You have never had cause for a moment's anxiety,
Yet,
In those great eyes of yours,
Those liquid and protuberant orbs,

Lies the shadow of immense insecurity. There
Panic walks.

Yes, yes, I know,
When your mistress is with you,
When your master
Takes you upon his lap,
Just then, for a moment,
Almost you are not frightened.

But at heart you are frightened, you always have been.
O Pug, obstinate old nervous breakdown,
In the midst of *so* much love,
*And* such comfort,
Still to feel unsafe and be afraid,

How one's heart goes out to you!

# NONE IS MORE FAITHFUL FOUND

'We judge the moral worth of two human friends according to which of them is ready to make the greater sacrifice without thought of recompense,' wrote the great ethologist Konrad Lorenz. 'The plain fact that my dog loves me more than I love him is undeniable and always fills me with a certain feeling of shame. The dog is ever ready to lay down his life for me.'

The readiness to lay down his life for a human friend is found in most dogs. They love more faithfully, more continuously and more unconditionally than we do. At our darkest moments they are with us – like the little dog which crept out from beneath the gown of the executed Mary, Queen of Scots 'yet afterwards would not departe from the dead corpse'.

Early historians were happy to acknowledge man's debt to the dog. The Roman historian, Pliny the Elder, recounts how the king of the Garamants was exiled but rescued 'by the means of two hundred dogs that fought for him against all those that made resistance, and brought him home maugre his enemies.' How lovely it would have been to see them after their successful military exploit – tongues hanging out, tails wagging like mad.

Many dogs have saved human lives. In Sir Walter Scott's diary, for November 1825, he recounted the story of Lord Forbes – 'that he was asleep in his house at Castle Forbes, when awakened by a sense of suffocation, which deprived him of the power of stirring a limb, yet left him the consciousness that the house was on fire. At this moment, and while his apartment was in flames, his large dog jumped on the bed, seized his shirt, and dragged him to the staircase, where the fresh air restored his powers of existence and of escape.'Most people know the story of Greyfriars Bobby, the dog who followed the body of his master to Greyfriars churchyard in 1858 and would not leave the grave side.

Even earlier is the story of a dog in ancient Rome, belonging to a man who was executed. When his master's corpse was thrown into the river Tiber, Pliny reported, 'The dog swam after, and made all the means he could to bear it up afloat that it should not sink: and to the sight of this spectacle and fidelity of the poor dog to his master, a number of people ran forth by heaps out of the city to the water side.'

Thousands of dogs still help us with their love. There are therapy dogs that visit the sick in hospitals or elderly people in homes, for dogs do not shy away from sickness, ugliness or old age. There are dogs that guide the blind, help the deaf, and assist the disabled. And dogs in the police force and in the army (though sadly no longer in special canine regiments!) still give their lives to protect their human handlers.

No wonder we love dogs – the wonder is that they love us!

William of Orange, leader of the Dutch revolt against King Philip II of Spain, owed his life to his dog. In 1572 a night attack was made upon his camp by the Spanish army led by Julian Romero. His dog woke him from slumber. For the rest of his life, the Prince kept a dog of the same kind and statues of him often show a little dog at his feet.

Julian…forced all the guards that he found in his way into the place of armes before the prince's tent. Here he entered divers tents; among the rest his men killed two of the prince's secretaries hard by the prince's tent, and the prince himself escaped very narrowly. For I heard the prince say often, that he thought, but for a dog he had been taken. The camisado was given with such resolution, that the place of armes took no alarme until their fellowes were running in with the enemies in their tailes: whereupon this dogge, hearing a great noyse, fell to scratching and crying, and withall leapt upon the prince's face, awaking him being asleepe, before any of his men. And albeit the prince lay in his armes, with a lackey alwaies holding one of his horses ready bridled, yet at the going out of his tent, with much adoe hee recovered his horse before the enemie arrived. Nevertheless one of his squires was slain taking horse presently after him, and divers of his servants were forced to escape amongst the guardes of foot, which could not recover their horses; for, in troth, ever since, untill the prince's dying day, he kept one of that dog's race; so did many of his friends and followers. The most or all of these dogs were white little hounds with crooked noses called camuses.

*Actions of the Low Countries,*
SIR ROGER WILLIAMS, 1618.

One of the earliest stories about the faithful nature of dogs is found in Homer's epic poem about Ulysses. Ulysses went off to fight with the Greeks besieging Troy and was away for twenty years. When he finally returned, nobody recognised him. His household all thought he must have perished on his travels. There was only one exception – his dog Argus. When Ulysses arrived at his home in the company of a shepherd Eumaeus, the dog was lying in the road at the entrance to the palace. Old and friendless without his master, he had lived the life of a street dog, lying at night on the midden tip, without anybody to care for him. Weakened with age and neglect the dog could only wag his tail and then, exhausted with the effort, died. Alexander Pope's translation tells the story.

## Ulysses And His Dog

Thus, near the gates conferring as they drew,
Argus, the dog, his ancient master knew;
He, not unconscious of the voice, and tread,
Lifts to the sound his ear, and rears his head.
Bred by Ulysses, nourished at his board,
But ah! not fated long to please his Lord!
To him, his swiftness and his strength were vain;
The voice of glory called him o'er the main.
Till then in every sylvan chase renowned,
With 'Argus, Argus', rung the woods around;
With him the youth pursued the goat or fawn,
Or traced the mazy leveret o'er the lawn.
Now left to man's ingratitude he lay,
Unhoused, neglected, in the public way;
And where on heaps the rich manure was spread,
Obscene with reptiles, took his sordid bed.

He knew his Lord; he knew, and strove to meet,
In vain he strove, to crawl and kiss his feet;
Yet (all he could) his tail, his ears, his eyes
Salute his master, and confess his joys.
Soft pity touched the mighty master's soul;
Adown his cheek a tear unbidden stole,
Stole unperceived; he turned his head, and dried
The drop humane: then thus impassioned cried:

'What noble beast in this abandoned state
Lies here all helpless at Ulysses' gate?
His bulk and beauty speak no vulgar praise;
If, as he seems, he *was* in better days,
Some care his age deserves: or was he prized
For worthless beauty? therefore now despised?
Such dogs, and men there are, mere things of state,
And always cherished by their friends, the Great.'

'Not Argus so,' (Eumaeus thus rejoined)
'But served a master of a nobler kind…
Now years unnerve him, and his lord is lost!…
The master gone, the servants what restrains?
Or dwells humanity where riot reigns?'

This said, the honest herdsman strode before:
The musing monarch pauses at the door:
The dog, whom fate had granted to behold
His Lord, when twenty tedious years had rolled,
Takes a last look, and having seen him, dies:
So closed for ever faithful Argus' eyes!

[29]

In 1876 an American court was treated to a beautiful speech about dogs by Senator George G. Vest. He was speaking to the jury in the trial of a Missouri man who had killed his neighbour's dog, which (it was claimed) had been worrying sheep.

The outcome of the case has been forgotten, but not the speech made by the Senator. It can be found in the *Congressional Record* of the *Second Session of the Sixty-Eighth Congress*, 20 January–7 February 1925. I am pleased it is in the official record. Dogs deserve no less.

Gentlemen of the jury, the best friend a man has in the world may turn against him and become his enemy. His son or daughter that he has reared with loving care may prove ungrateful. Those who are nearest and dearest to us, those whom we trust with our happiness and good name may become traitors to their faith. The money that a man has he may lose... A man's reputation may be sacrificed in a moment of ill-considered action. The people who are prone to fall on their knees to do us honour when success is with us may be the first to throw the stone of malice when failure settles its clouds upon our heads.

The one absolutely unselfish friend that a man can have in this selfish world, the one that never deserts him, the one that never proves ungrateful or treacherous, is his dog. He will sleep on the cold ground where the wintry winds blow and the snow drives fiercely if only he may be near his master's side. He will kiss the hand that has no food to offer. He will lick the wounds and sores that come in encounter with the roughness of the world. He guards the sleep of his pauper master as if he were a prince. When all other friends desert he remains. When riches take wings and reputation falls to pieces he is as constant in his love as the sun in its journey through the heaven. If fortune drives the master forth an outcast in the world, the faithful dog asks no higher privilege than that of accompanying him, to guard against danger, to fight his enemies.

One of the first English books giving instructions on how to keep dogs was written by Edmund de Langley, Duke of York, in the fourteenth century. The book is about hunting, but there is a particularly moving passage which comes from the chapter 'Of ye Manners and Tatches and condicions of Hounds'. 'Tatches' is an old word for 'sagacity'. Much of what he says is exactly what dog-owners know to be true today.

An hounde is trewe to his lord or his maystere, and of good love and vrey [truth]. An hounde is of greet undirstondying and of great knowyinge, a hound is of greet strength and greete bounte, an hounde is a wise beast and a kynde, an hounde hath greet mynde and greet smellyng, an hounde hath grete bisynesse and greet mygt, an hounde is of greet wurthyness and of great sotilte, a hound is of greet ligtnesse and of greet purueaunce [perception], an hounde is of good obeysaunce for he wil lerne as a man al that a man will teche hym, a hounde is ful of good sport… Houndes ben hardy for oon hounde dar wel kepe his maister's hous and his beests and also he wil kepe all his maister's goodes and rathe [rather] he wil be dede yan eny thing be lost in his kepyng.

On the wall of Ditchley House, a stately home in Oxfordshire, is the portrait of Sir Henry Lee and his dog, Bevis. Sir Henry has his right hand on the head of Bevis who is wearing a leather collar and was said to be a Cheshire mastiff, though he looks a little like a large foxhound. On his collar is the inscription 'More true than favoured'.

Bevis was normally hardly noticed by his master. Yet one evening he accompanied his master to bed, crawled under the bed and could not be driven out. At length Sir Henry ordered him to be left there. That night a treacherous servant entered the room in order to murder and rob Sir Henry. He was seized by Bevis and confessed all.

Sir Henry had his portrait painted with Bevis by Marcus Gheeraerts the Younger probably around the time of 1592. A verse is inscribed upon the portrait, in which Sir Henry compares himself to Ulysses.

Reason in man cannot effect such love,
As nature doth in them that reason want;
Ulysses true and kind his dog did prove,
When faith in better friends was very scante.
My travailes for my friends have been as true,
Though not as far as fortune did him bear;
No friende my love and faith devided knewe,
Though neyither this nor that once equalde were.
Onely my dog, whereof I made no store,
I find more love, then them I trusted more.

One of the loveliest tributes to the dog came from Maurice Maeterlinck, the Belgian poet and playwright who died in 1949.

Man loves the dog, but how much more ought he to love it... We are alone, absolutely alone, on this chance planet; and, amid all the forms of life that surround us, not one, excepting the dog, has made an alliance with us. A few creatures fear us, most are unaware of us and not one loves us... Now in this indifference and this total want of comprehension amid which all that surrounds us lives; in this incommunicable world, where everything has its object hermetically contained within itself, where every destiny is self-circumscribed, where exist among created things no other relations than those of executioners and victims, eaters and eaten, ...where death alone establishes cruel relations of cause and effect between neighbouring lives, where not the smallest sympathy has ever made a conscious leap from one species to another, one animal alone, among all that breathes upon the earth, has succeeded in breaking through the prophetic circle, in escaping from itself to come bounding towards us, in definitely crossing the enormous zone of darkness, ice and silence that isolates each category of existence in nature's unintelligible plan. This animal, our good familiar dog, simple and unsurprising as may today appear to us what he has done, in thus perceptibly drawing nearer to a world in which he was not born and for which he was not destined, has nevertheless performed one of the most unusual and improbable acts that we can find in the general history of life ... We have not to gain his confidence or his friendship: he is born our friend; while his eyes are still closed, already he believes in us: even before his birth, he has given himself to man.

It is said that dogs are despised in Arab countries. Even so, there have been Arabs who valued their courage and fidelity. An Arab writer, Ibn al-Marzuban, wrote a book called *Fadl al-Kilab*, splendidly translated as, *The Book of the Superiority of Dogs over Those Who Wear Clothes*. It is a collection of sayings and poems about dogs, many of them proving that dogs are more faithful and reliable than human beings. Ibn al-Marzuban was writing in the tenth century and this is his most famous book. The last two lines are about the Arab custom of finding your way in the desert – if you are lost, you imitate the barking of a dog and the local bedouin dogs bark back. By following the noise they make, you find your way to their camp.

## O You Who Hate Dogs

O you who hate dogs! Listen to me:
    pay attention and do not close your mind to what I say.
The dog – note well – is reckoned
    to have five noble qualities:
He protects those who are good to him; he shows loyalty
    to those who keep him for the hunt and for guarding;
He keeps an eye on his master's baggage, even when
    brave men are afraid to speak out.
He is a help to the man who imitates barking from afar,
    seeking protection from the nearness of the dog, when evening
    comes.

Every time we arrive home, our dogs are delighted. They are never too busy to come and say hello, never too self-concerned to greet us with wagging tails, always spontaneous in their pleasure at seeing us. In 1709 the essayist Richard Steele wrote about the pleasures of owning two animal friends, a cat and a dog, in his town house.

For my own part, I am excluded all conversation with animals that delight only in a country life, and am therefore forced to entertain myself as well as I can with my little dog and cat. They both of them sit by my fire every night, expecting my coming home with impatience; and at my entrance, never fail of running up to me, and bidding me welcome, each of them in his proper language. As they have been bred up together from their infancy, and seen no other company, they have learned each other's manners, so that the dog often gives himself the airs of a cat, and the cat, in several of her motions and gestures, affects the behaviour of the little dog. When they are at play, I often make one with them; and sometimes please myself with considering, how much reason and instinct are capable of delighting each other.

## None Is More Faithful Found

Of any beast, none is more faithful found,
Nor yields more pastime in house, plain, or woods,
Nor keeps his master's person, nor his goods,
With greater care, than doth the dog or hound.

Command: he thee obeys most readily.
Strike him: he whines and falls down at thy feet.
Call him: he leaves his game and comes to thee
With wagging tail, off'ring his service meek.

In summer's heat he follows by thy pace:
In winter's cold he never leaveth thee:
In mountains wild he by thee close doth trace;
In all thy fears and dangers true is he.

Thy friends he loves; and in thy presence lives
By day: by night he watcheth faithfully
That thou in peace may sleep: he never gives
Good entertainment to thine enemy.

Canst thou then such a creature hate and spurn?
Or bar him from such poor and simple food?
Being so fit and faithful for thy turn,
As no beast else can do thee half such good.

JAMES MICYLLUS

I will leave it to Jerome K. Jerome, author of *Three Men in a Boat* and owner of Montmorency, to have the last word on the fidelity and devotion of dogs.

I like cats and dogs very much indeed. What jolly chaps they are! they are much superior to human beings as companions. They do not quarrel or argue with you. They never talk about themselves, but listen to you while you talk about yourself, and keep up an appearance of being interested in the conversation. They never say unkind things. They never tell us of our faults 'merely for our own good'. They do not, at inconvenient moments, remind us of our past follies and mistakes. They never inform us that we are not nearly so nice as we used to be. We are always the same to them. They are always glad to see us. They are with us in all our humours. They are merry when we are glad, sober when we feel solemn, sad when we are sorrowful…

And when we bury our face in our hands and wish we had never been born, they don't sit up very straight, and observe that we have brought it all upon ourselves. They don't even hope it will be a warning to us.

But they come up softly; and shove their heads against us. If it is a dog, he looks up at you with his big, true eyes, and says with them, 'Well, you've always got me, you know. We'll go through the world together, and always stand by each other, won't we?'

He is very imprudent, a dog is. He never makes it his business to inquire whether you are in the right or in the wrong, never bothers as to whether you are going up or down upon life's ladder, never asks whether you are rich or poor, silly or wise, sinner or saint. Come luck or misfortune, good repute or bad, honour or shame, he is going to stick to you, to comfort you, guard you, and give his life for you, if need be… You are his pal. That is enough for him.

# CLEVER CANINES

Because dogs cannot talk we sometimes call them our 'dumb' friends. Yet they are wonderfully expressive. Look into a dog's eyes and he will tell you all kinds of things – ranging from 'I love you so much' to 'Why can't I chase that cat?' to 'I am really dying for that piece of biscuit'.

Dogs understand us only too well. They know, as their anxious looks tell us, when we are going to go away on holiday. They sense that we are thinking of taking them for a walk. They read our moods, offering comfort at one moment and at the next a playful invitation to have fun. Besides, they have their own canine talents and intelligence. We can read books but a dog can sniff a book and 'read' who last handled it. We can enjoy and make clever remarks about a sunset, yet a dog can walk down a suburban street and find a world of smells unnoticed by us. Indeed researchers in France are investigating a possibility that dogs may even be able to detect the mood of a person purely by smell.

Moreover, though dogs may not be able to speak, they can certainly recognise many of our words. In 1789 Horace Walpole, the English man of letters, wrote perceptively: 'I must celebrate the sense of Fidelle, Mrs Damer's terrier. Without making the slightest gesture, her mistress only said to her, "Now, Fidelle, you may here jump on any chair you please"; she instantly jumped on the settee; and so she did in every room for the whole two days she stayed. This is another demonstration to me that dogs understand even language as far as it relates to their own affairs.'

Dogs are not stupid. 'They have what's known as delayed memory,' says Dr Valerie Farrell, clinical psychologist and dog behaviour expert at Edinburgh University's veterinary school. 'If you put two cups down on the floor with a titbit under one of them and show this to the dog, it will remember it. You can take it away for quite some time, and it will remember when it comes back into the room.'

In literature about dogs there are many examples of startlingly bright canines. Sir Walter Scott's bull terrier, Camp, for instance, not only understood 'a great many words' but having once been beaten for biting the baker, used to retreat into the corner of the room every time the man was mentioned. In this chapter there are examples of dogs who seem to have been able to understand and puzzle out a problem.

Doting owners, however, sometimes expect too much of their pets. Elizabeth Barrett Browning tried, without success, to teach her spaniel Flush to count. She hoped that one day he might play dominoes with her. The painter Philip Reinagle painted his dog at the keyboard of a piano, though it seems unlikely the dog could actually play the instrument.

As for the dogs, themselves, they will always try to please their owners by doing tricks: they will also enjoy showing these off. But perhaps the real talent of dogs is not to be bright, but to be good. At the end of this chapter is a poem by the Elizabethan satirist John Marston about his spaniel who knew the folly of being too clever.

# Letters from Elizabeth Barrett Browning

*22 November 1843*

By the way my Flush learnt to count to *three*, in ten minutes yesterday.

*27-28 November 1843*

Flushie's arithmetic is less complex than you & Ben imagine. I hold up a piece of cake, & say one, two, three; and after 'three', & not sooner, he takes it. It is amusing to see him stir his little head at 'two' & then correct himself – and still more amusing to observe how, at every unqualified success, he turns round and looks… for applause. Are you aware of the existence of a M. Leonard who… has educated two dogs which he carries about with him. The Athenaeum did him two years ago the honour of a notice, & an acknowledgement… & were very nearly satisfied of there being no shadow of a 'trick' in them. The Athenaeum proposed several hard words, which the dogs spelt, and one or two sums, I believe, which they calculated, – & finished these graver studies with a game at dominoes, which was won by the dogs…

Now I am jealous of Mr Leonard's dogs – & I can't help it. Therefore, you see, I begin arithmetic with Flushie, – and am trying to teach him his letters, … with a 'Kiss **A**, Flush – and now kiss **B**'. I am afraid nevertheless that he has no very pronounced love for literature & that there is a possibility of my failing to inspire it.

John Clare was the uneducated son of a farm worker near Peterborough. Yet he wrote some of the finest poems in the English language. This poem about his dog, Rover, was written between 1808 and 1819.

## My Rover

Who nightly in his den does lye
That slumbers only with one eye
And barks if any thing stirs nigh
My Rover

Who finds me out both far and near,
Tracing my footsteps every where
And when I wistle's sure to hear
My Rover

Who will himself from day to day
Tend sheep so well when I'm away
As not to let one go astray
   My Rover

Who  stands upon his under legs
And wistful on his master glegs
To show me how genteel he begs
   My Rover

And who when I at dinner sit
In silence seems to beg a bit
Then wags his tail in thanks for it
   My Rover

Who oer me such a watch will keep
As flies themselves dare hardley creep
To bit me when I fall asleep
   My Rover

And who to please me with a trick
Will carry in his mouth a stick
Or any thing that's not too thick
   My Rover

Nay I need not no further go
For everything in short that you
Can please me with thoult freeley do
   My Rover

During the last century it was the fashion to collect anecdotes of remarkable animals. The Reverend William Bingley, a natural history writer and author of *Animal Biography* at the beginning of the nineteenth century, devoted pages to the cleverness of dogs.

It is recorded of a Dog belonging to a nobleman of the Medici family, that it always attended at its master's table; changed the plates for him; and carried him his wine in a glass placed on a salver without spilling the smallest drop. This animal would also hold the stirrup in its teeth while its master was mounting his horse.

The sagacity and attention of the Dog are, indeed, so great, that it is not difficult to teach him to dance, hunt, leap and exhibit a thousand pleasing dexterities. The feats performed by the dancing dogs exhibited some years ago at Sadler's Wells, will be long remembered. After storming a fort, and performing various other exploits, one of them was brought in as a deserter, was shot, and carried off as dead by his companions...

But of all the educational attainments by which the Dog has been distinguished, that of learning to speak seems to be the most extraordinary. The French academicians, however, mention a Dog in Germany, which would call, in an intelligible manner, amongst other things, for tea, coffee, or chocolate. This Dog was of a middling size and the property of a peasant in Saxony. A little boy, the peasant's son, imagined that he perceived in the Dog's voice an indistinct resemblance to certain words, and therefore took it into his head to teach him to speak...at length he made such progress in language, as to be able to articulate as many as thirty words.

One of the most moving books written about an individual dog was *Memories* by John Galsworthy. It tells the story of his much-loved black spaniel, Chris. Chris was really a gun dog but Galsworthy gave up shooting because he could not bear to slaughter birds. Instead of retrieving game, Chris played cricket – a game which Englishmen take very seriously indeed.

I often felt, and especially when we heard guns, how the best and most secret instincts of him were being stifled. Yet always, even in his most cossetted and idle days, he managed to preserve the grave preoccupation of one professionally concerned with retrieving things that smell; and consoled himself with pastimes such as cricket, which he played in a manner highly specialized, following the ball up the moment it left the bowler's hand, and sometimes retrieving it before it reached the batsman. When remonstrated with, he would consider a little, hanging out a pink tongue and looking rather too eagerly at the ball, then canter slowly out to a sort of forward short leg. Why he always chose that particular position it is difficult to say; possibly he could lurk there better than anywhere else, the batsman's eye not being on him, and the bowler's not too much… But he worked tremendously, watching every movement; for he knew the game thoroughly, and seldom delayed it more than three minutes when he secured the ball. And if that ball were really lost, then indeed he took over the proceedings with an intensity and quiet vigour that destroyed many shrubs, and the solemn satisfaction which comes from being in the very centre of the stage.

Devoted owners cannot resist boasting about their dogs. One such was Sir John Harington, a soldier, a poet and the godson of Queen Elizabeth I. On 14 June 1608, Sir John wrote this letter to Prince Henry, then heir to the British throne and the son of James I, telling the story of Bungey. Clearly Sir John was bursting with pride about Bungey's exploits.

Havinge goode reason to thinke your Highnesse had goode will and likinge to reade what others have told of my rare Dogge, I will even give a brief historie of his good deedes and straunge feats... I did once relate to your Highnesse after what sort his tacklinge was, wherewithe he did sojourn from my house at the Bathe to Greenwiche Palace, and deliver up to the court there such matters as were entrusted to his care. This he hathe often done, and come safe to the Bathe, or my house here at Kelstone, with goodly returnes from such nobilitie as were pleased to emploie him...

Neither must it be forgotten as how he once was sente with two charges of sack wine from the Bathe to my house by my man Combe; and on his way the cordage did slacken; but my trustie bearer did now bear himselfe so wisely as to covertly hide one flasket in the rushes, and take the other in his teethe to the house; after which he went forthe and returnede with the other parte of his burden to dinner...

I neede not saie how muche I did once grieve at missing this Dogge: for on my journie towards Londonne, some idle pastimers did diverte themselves with hunting mallardes in a pond, and conveyed him to the Spanish ambassador's; where (in a happie hour) after six weekes I did heare of him; but such was the court he did pay to the Don, that he was no less in good likinge there than at home. Nor did the householde listen to any claim or challenge, till I rested my suite on the Dogge's own proofes, and made him perform such feates before the nobles assembled, as put it past doubt that I was his master. I did send him to the hall in the time of dinner, and made him bring thence a pheasant out of the dish, which created much mirthe; but much more, when he returned at my commandment and put it again in the same cover. Herewith the company was well content to allow me my claim, and we both were well content to accept it, and came homewards…

Now let Ulysses praise his Dogge Argus, or Tobit be led by that Dogge whose name doth not appear; yet coud I say such things of my Bungey (for so was he styled) as might shame them both, either for good faith, clear wit, or wonderful deedes; to say no more than I have said, of his bearing letters to London and Greenwiche, more than an hundred miles. As I doubt not but your Highness would love my Dogge, if not myself, I have been thus tedious in his story; and again say, that of all the Dogges near your father's court, not one hath more love, more diligence to please, or less pay for pleasing than him I write of; for verily a bone would contente my servante, when some expecte greater matters…

In the shooting season a special companionship occurs between man and dog. Just seeing the gun, will make a good gun dog tremble with excitement. I have often heard shooters complain of the mortifying behaviour of their dogs during a day's sport. But how do the dogs feel about human behaviour among the guns? I expect that when the labradors, setters and retrievers get together at the end of the day, that they complain in much the same way about humans.

Occasionally, very occasionally, a gun dog, unable to bear his owner's incompetent behaviour any longer, makes his feelings known. In an old book, *Rural Sports*, by W.B. Daniel, published as long ago as 1805, I found this charming little anecdote (which is also a concealed bit of sportsman's boasting!) about the gun dog who was ashamed of his master's poor shooting.

A setter, to whom I had shot for three seasons, once left me when shooting in a country distant from home, and returned to the inn which we had set out from that morning. I had fired seven or eight times without dropping a bird, and have no doubt but my want of skill occasioned Sancho's distaste; for, after riding back to the inn, and again taking him to the field, he soon gave me an opportunity of regaining his confidence, and for seventeen successive shots, not a bird was missed. A perfect reconciliation was the consequence.

Sometimes when I look at a dog asleep I envy its serenity. Animals have a better grasp of life's real priorities. This poem by John Marston is about a spaniel who was a true philosopher.

## The Scholar's Dog

I was a scholar: seven useful springs
Did I deflower in quotations
Of crossed opinions 'bout the soul of man;
The more I learnt, the more I learnt to doubt.
'Delight', my spaniel, slept whilst I baused leaves,
Tossed o'er the dunces, pored on the old print
Of titled words: *and still my spaniel slept.*
Whilst I wasted lamp-oil, baited my flesh,
Shrunk up my veins: *and still my spaniel slept.*
And still I held converse with Zabarell,
Aquinas, Scotus, and the musty saws
Of antique Donate: *still my spaniel slept.*
Still on went I; first, 'an sit anima';
Then, an it were mortal. O hold, hold! at that
They're at brain buffets, fell by the ears amain
Pell-mell together: *still my spaniel slept.*
Then, whether 'twere corporeal, local, fixed,
'Ex traduce'; but whether 't had free will
Or no, hot philosophers
Stood banding factions, all so strongly propped;
I staggered, knew not which was firmer part,
But thought, quoted, read, observed, and pried,
Stuffed noting-books: *and still my spaniel slept.*
At length he waked, and yawned; and by yon sky,
For aught I know, he knew as much as I.

# FOOD, FLEAS, LOVE, AND OTHER DISAGREEMENTS

The course of true love, even that of a man for his dog, never did run smooth. When you consider how often men and women are at cross purposes, no wonder that sometimes a vast misunderstanding should arise between two different species. Food, love, fleas, and baths are all matters on which dogs and human beings have rather different ideas and it is not always the human point of view that triumphs.

Some dogs take shameless advantage of devoted owners. The mother of cartoonist and writer James Thurber had an Airedale called Muggs that bit people. Every Christmas this old lady would send propitiatory boxes of chocolates to the dog's victims until, by the end of Muggs' eleven years of life, there were forty names on her Christmas shopping list.

Strong-minded dogs naturally cling to their own ideas about what constitutes proper behaviour. The poet Walter Savage Landor wrote to a friend about his white Pomeranian, Pomero. 'Last evening I look him to hear Luisa de Sodre play and sing. Pomero was deeply affected, and lay close to the pedal on her gown, singing in a great variety of tones, not always in time. It is unfortunate that he always *will* take a part where there is music, for he sings even worse than I do.'

Almost all dogs have a firm conviction that a dog should smell doggy and their idea of an additional perfume is a rotting carcase, on which they carefully roll. Dogs also know that fleas are part of the canine condition – they provide leisurely sport when there is nothing better to do. It is only unreasonable humans, with their warped sense of smell, that insist on baths, flea powders and (in California) special pet shop perfumes.

At other times trouble arises because of tensions within the family. It is not that dogs misunderstand what is going on: they understand all too well. Elizabeth Barrett Browning's spaniel Flush seems to have sensed the potential threat of Mr Barrett, her Victorian father. If Papa Barrett asked him to come downstairs with him, Flush used to run away as if pursued by demons. Everybody in the family would laugh and Mr Barrett would call Flush a fool. But it seems to me that Flush was probably correctly sensing what a threat Mr Barrett's solicitude was to his daughter's happiness.

Human beings can be unfair. Ill-feeling between humans is often taken out on dogs – hate me, hate my dog, as it were. Several thwarted lovers have written bitter poems complaining of their sweetheart's preference for a lapdog. Other moments of tension, discord and misunderstanding are recorded in dog literature.

There is, however, one major difference between men and dogs. Dogs never bear grudges. 'You tread on his tail or foot, he expresses, for a moment, the uneasiness of his feelings, but in a moment the complaint is ended,' wrote John Wolcot, an eighteenth-century writer. 'He runs around you; jumps up against you, seems to declare his sorrow for complaining, as it was not intentionally done; and begs, by whinings and lickings, that master will think of it no more.' If to err is human, then to forgive is canine.

The worst behaved dog in English literature is Crab, the dog belonging to servant Launce in Shakespeare's play *The Two Gentlemen of Verona*.

## Launce's Soliloquy

When a man's servant shall play the cur with him, look you, it goes hard: one that I brought up of a puppy; one that I saved from drowning, when three or four of his blind brothers and sisters went to it! I was sent to deliver him as a present to Mistress Silvia from my master, and I came no sooner into the dining chamber, but he steps me to her trencher and steals her capon's leg; O, 'tis a foul thing when a cur cannot keep himself in all companies! If I had not had more wit than he, to take a fault upon me that he did, I think verily he had been hanged for't; sure as I live, he had suffered for't: you shall judge. He thrusts me himself into the company of three or four gentlemanlike dogs under the duke's table: he had not been there – bless the mark – a pissing while, but all the chamber smelt him. 'Out with the dog!' says one: 'What cur is that?' says another: 'Whip him out,' says the third; 'Hang him up,' says the duke. I, having been acquainted with the smell before, knew it was Crab, and goes me to the fellow that whips the dogs: 'Friend,' quoth I, 'you mean to whip the dog?' 'Ay, marry, do I,' quoth he. 'You do him the more wrong,' quoth I: 'twas I did the thing you wot of.' He makes me no more ado, but whips me out of the chamber. How many masters would do this for his servant? Nay, I'll be sworn, I have sat in the stocks for puddings he hath stolen, otherwise he had been executed; I have stood on the pillory for geese he hath killed, otherwise he had suffered for't. Thou thinkest not of this now. Nay, I remember the trick you served me when I took my leave of Madam Silvia: did not I bid thee still mark me, and do as I do? when didst thou see me heave up my leg, and make water against a gentlewoman's farthingale? didst thou ever see me do such a trick?

There are moments when our dogs embarrass us dreadfully. I was amused to find these entries in the diary of Parson James Woodforde. He lived with his sister, Nancy, and a series of dogs. In the first diary entry he refers to 'charter' which may have been some special dish.

## Parson Woodforde's Diary

*10 August l786*
Nancy and self very busy this morning in making the Charter having some Company to dine with us – but unfortunately the cellar door being left open whilst it was put in there to cool, one of the Greyhounds (by name Jigg) got in and eat the whole, with a Cold Tongue etc. Sister Pounsett & Nancy mortally vexed at it.

*28 August l787*
My Greyhounds being both very full of fleas & almost raw on their backs, I put some Oil of Turpentine on them.

*11 April l794*
One of my Greyhounds, young Fly, got to Betty Cary's this morning and ran away with a Shoulder of Mutton undressed & eat it all up. They made great lamentation & work about it.

*1 August l796*
We returned home by Weston House, got out there and walked down to the garden, where unluckily My Dog Ranger killed a favourite Cat of Knight's.

I know of several love poems in which a lover complains about his mistress's preference for a dog. Sir Philip Sidney, the Elizabethan poet and statesman, wrote one of the best. I think Sir Philip is unfair to the dog – claiming that it is witless and that its breath smells!

Perhaps Stella, his mistress, was teasing her lover deliberately. She seems to have cuddled her dog, allowed it to 'clip', i.e. embrace her, and even let it lick her on the lips, in front of him. Not really kind behaviour to her fellow human, though I dare say the dog rather enjoyed showing off in front of his rival.

## From Astrophel and Stella

Dear, why make you more of a dog than me?
  If he do love, I burn, I burn in love:
  If he wait well, I never thence would move:
If he be fair, yet but a dog can be.
Little he is, so little worth is he;
  He barks, my songs thine own voice oft doth prove;
  Bidden perhaps he fetcheth thee a glove,
But I unbid, fetch even my soul to thee.
  Yet while I languish, him that bosom clips,
That lap doth lap, nay lets in spite of spite,
This sour-breathed mate taste of those sugared lips.
Alas, if you grant only such delight
  To witless things, then Love, I hope (since wit
  Becomes a clog) will soon ease me of it.

Some dogs have their owners completely under their paw. Wessex, a wire-haired terrier belonging to Thomas Hardy, was one of these. He slept on the sofa. He bit the postman three times. He bit John Galsworthy once. Worse still, he would jump up on the table while guests were dining with the Hardys and try to take the food off their fork. The playwright J.M. Barrie reveals how Wessex monopolised Hardy's radio, then called 'a broadcasting set'. Just as today's dogs have their favourites on television, so Wessex had his favourite radio programmes.

> Once when I was at Dorchester, he showed me a letter from a firm which had presented him with a broadcasting set. They said they were delighted to hear from him that it gave pleasure, but that they were rather damped to learn from another source that it was not he who listened but his dog. This was quite true.
>
> We went that afternoon to a local rehearsal of the play of *Tess*, and the dog, who was with us, behaved beautifully until the time came when he knew the wireless would be putting on the Children's Hour. It was his favourite item. He howled for it so that even Tess's champion had to desert her and hurry home with him.
>
> The dog afterwards discovered that a weather report, or something of the kind, was issued in the early morning, and I understand his master used to go downstairs in the cold and turn it on for him.

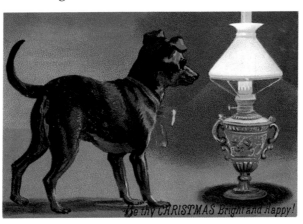

Be thy CHRISTMAS Bright and Happy!

Dogs can cause dissent within the family. In family rows, one person often sides with the dog while the other is against it. There's a rather nice poem about this by Sir John Harington, the same man who wrote to Prince Henry about his clever dog Bungey. It is his wife's dog, not Bungey, which is the subject of this poem.

Sir John Harington must have been a good husband and a dog-lover. He was not ashamed to say sorry. The last line is a reference to an old proverb, 'Beat the dog to frighten the lion', i.e. frighten the stronger one by punishing the weaker.

## To His Wife, For Striking Her Dog

Your little dog that barked as I came by,
I strake by hap so hard, I made him cry,
And straight you put your finger in
    your eye
And low'ring sat. I asked the reason
    why.
'Love me and love my dog,' thou didst
    reply:
'Love, as both should be loved.' 'I will,'
    said I,
And sealed it with a kiss. Then by and
    by
Cleared were the clouds of thy fair
    frowning sky;
Thus small events great masteries may
    try.
For I by this, do at their meaning
    guess,
    That beat a whelp afore a lioness.

[57]

Hard-hearted people often take the view that it is not right to get too fond of dogs. Embittered men seem particularly censorious about women loving small dogs. An early example of this comes in *A Treatise of English Dogges* by John Caius in 1576. He has unkind words to say about 'the spaniel gentle'. I would not have included his diatribe except that he reveals (somewhat against his will) that they were useful as hot water bottles.

## Of the Delicate, Neat and Pretty Kind of Dogs Called the Spaniel Gentle or the Comforter

These dogs are little, pretty, proper, and fine, and sought for to satisfy the delicateness of dainty dames, and wanton women's wills, instruments of folly for them to play and dally withall, to trifle away the treasure of time, to withdraw their mindes from more commendable exercises, and to content their corrupted concupiscences with vain disport. These puppies the smaller they be, the more pleasure they provoke, as more meet playfellows for mincing mistresses to bear in their bosoms, to keep company withall in their chambers, to succour with sleep in bed, and nourish with meat at board, to lay in their laps, and lick their lips as they ride in their waggons…

And though some suppose that such dogs are right for no service, I dare say, by their leaves, they be in a wrong box… We find that these little dogs are good to assuage sickness of the stomach, being oftentimes thereunto applied as a plaster preservative, or born in the bosom of the diseased and weak person, which effect is performed by their moderate heat.

[58]

Some humans commission a portrait of their dog, just as they might have portraits done of other family members – a custom inexplicable to dogs. The poet Jonathan Swift wrote some not entirely serious lines to a portrait painter in praise of a spaniel.

Instructions to a Painter

Happiest of the spaniel race,
Painter, with thy colours grace;
Draw his forehead large and high,
Draw his blue and humid eye;
Draw his neck so smooth and round,
Little neck with ribands bound;
And the musely swelling breast
Where the loves and graces rest;
And the spreading even back,
Soft, and sleek, and glossy black;
And the tail that gentle twines,
Like the tendrils of the vines;
And the silky twisted hair,
Shadowing thick the velvet ear;
Velvet ears, which, hanging low,
O'er the veiny temples flow…

An understanding view of dogs comes from the naturalist Charles Darwin, the man who first put forward the theory of evolution. In his book, *The Expression of the Emotions in Man and Animals*, Darwin described what we should call the body language of dogs.

He set a good example, which unfortunately many subsequent scientists ignored. He studied the family dog to confirm his theories. He did not cut it up or put it in a cage or make it run a maze – he simply observed it in his natural surroundings, in this case, his own family.

I formerly possessed a large dog, who, like every other dog, was much pleased to go out walking. He showed his pleasure by trotting gravely before me with high steps, head much raised, moderately

erected ears, and tail carried aloft but not stiffly. Not far from my house a path branches off to the right, leading to the hot-house, which I used often to visit for a few moments, to look at my experimental plants. This was always a great disappointment to the dog, as he did not know whether I should continue my walk; and the instantaneous and complete change of expression which came over him as soon as my body swerved in the least towards the path (and I sometimes tried this as an experiment) was laughable. His look of dejection was known to every member of the family, and was called his *hot-house face*. This consisted in the head drooping much, the whole body sinking a little and remaining motionless; the ears and tail falling suddenly down, but the tail was by no means wagged. With the falling of the ears and of his great chaps, the eyes became much changed in appearance, and I fancied that they looked less bright. His aspect was that of piteous hopeless dejection; and it was, as I have said, laughable, as the cause was so slight...

When two young dogs in play are growling and biting each other's faces and legs, it is obvious that they mutually understand each other's gestures and manners. There seems, indeed, some degree of instinctive knowledge in puppies and kittens, that they must not use their sharp little teeth or claws too freely in their play. When my terrier bites my hand in play, often snarling at the same time, if he bites too hard and I say *gently, gently*, he goes on biting, but answers me by a few wags of the tail, which seems to say 'Never mind, it is all fun.'...

A pleasurable and excited state of mind, associated with affection is exhibited by some dogs in a very peculiar manner; namely by grinning. Some persons speak of the grin as a smile, but if it had been really a smile, we should see a similar, though more pronounced, movement of the lips and ears, when dogs utter their bark of joy; but this is not the case, although a bark of joy often follows a grin.

From the playwright J.M. Barrie, author of *Peter Pan*, comes the best description of a dog getting his own way by eye power. Barrie's St Bernard was called Porthos, a dog so gentle that he would tiptoe up to rabbits and give them a kind of nudge with his nose! Barrie used to buy him toys (from a human toyshop) which the dog took to bed with him and sometimes swallowed whole. He also gave Porthos a Christmas present to unwrap every year. Porthos and his successor, a Newfoundland called Luath, were the inspiration for Nana, the dog that looks after the children in the nursery, in *Peter Pan*.

A score of times I have told him that he had much better not come; I have announced fiercely that he is not to come. He then lets go of his legs, which is how a St Bernard sits down, making the noise of a sack of coals suddenly deposited, and, laying his head between his front paws, stares at me through the red haws that make his eyes so mournful. He will do this for an hour without blinking, for he knows that in time it will unman me. My dog knows very little, but what little he does know he knows extraordinarily well. One can get out of my chambers by a back way, and I sometimes steal softly – but I can't help looking back, and there he is, and there are those haws asking sorrowfully, 'Is this worthy of you?'

'Curse you,' I say, 'get your hat,' or words to that effect...

The eighteenth-century poet William Cowper wrote this charming poem addressed to his spaniel Beau, who had killed a fledgeling.

## Beau and the Bird

A spaniel, Beau, that fares like you,
Well fed, and at his ease,
Should wiser be than to pursue
Each trifle that he sees.

But you have killed a tiny bird
Which flew not till today,
Against my orders, whom you heard
Forbidding you the prey.

Nor did you kill that you might eat,
And ease a doggish pain,
For him, though chased with furious heat,
You left where he was slain.

Nor was he of the thievish
    sort,
Or one whom blood allures,
But innocent was all his sport
Whom you have torn for yours.

My dog! What remedy remains,
Since, teach you all I can,
I see you, after all my pains,
So much resemble man?

A second poem by Cowper is Beau's justification for his misdeed. Poor Cowper! In 1796 Beau died of old age and was stuffed. One of Cowper's friends said he hoped that the stuffed dog might 'make a pleasing and salutary impression on the poet's reviving fancy'. It is difficult to see how it could have cheered up the poet, who was sunk in deep depression at the time. These verses, supposedly written by Beau while the dog was still living, show the poet's tender empathy with his dog.

## Beau's Reply

Sir, when I flew to seize the bird
In spite of your command,
A louder voice than yours I heard,
And harder to withstand.

You cried 'Forbear', but in my breast
A mightier cried 'Proceed'.
'Twas nature, sir, whose strong behest
Impelled me to the deed.

Yet much as nature I respect,
I ventured once to break
(As you perhaps may recollect)
Her precept for your sake;

And when your linnet on a day
Passing his prison door,
Had fluttered all his strength away,
And panting pressed the floor,

Well knowing him a sacred thing,
Not destined to my tooth,
I only kissed his ruffled wing
And licked the feathers smooth.

Let my obedience then excuse
My disobedience now,
Nor some reproof yourself refuse
From your aggrieved Bow-wow.

If killing birds be such a crime
(Which I can hardly see),
What think you, sir, of killing time
With verse addressed to me?

# IN SORROW AND IN TEARS

There is no happy ending in the love between man and dog. All relationships end in mourning, for a dog's life-span is, at best, only one fifth of a human's. We part in sorrow and in tears and there is no other way. Real love brings both joy and woe. We cannot have the joy without the eventual woe.

'The misery of keeping a dog is his dying so soon,' wrote Sir Walter Scott. 'But, to be sure, if he lived for 50 years and then died, what would become of me?' We dog-lovers know that the misery will come only too soon, but to turn aside from love, because it brings pain as well as pleasure, is to live only half a life.

Mourning a dog is the same as mourning a person. There is the same disbelief, a feeling of unreality, about the death. We expect to hear those feet trotting behind us. We look round and the house is empty. Our companion of so many hours is missing. It is hard to believe it could have happened, that a being so loved and so loving no longer exists. If we are unlucky, some insensitive acquaintance will tell us: 'It was only a dog.' Or a thoughtless friend will try to cheer us up with: 'Why not get another one?'

Perhaps it is the world's indifference to the death of a pet dog that has produced so much moving poetry on the subject. Minor poets like William

Watson rise to unusual heights. Great poets like Lord Byron and William Wordsworth are full of feeling on the subject.

The determination that the loved being shall not be forgotten, shall not be ignored as a 'mere dog', goes deep. Tombs dedicated to dogs have been found from earliest times. One ancient Greek epitaph reads: 'You who pass by, if you do mark this monument, do not laugh, I beg you, though it is a dog's grave. Tears fell for me, and the earth was heaped above me by a master's hand, who likewise engraved these words on my tomb.'

Each tombstone and each epitaph is, I think, a protest against death, a moment of defiance against the fate which rules that both dog and man must end forgotten in the dust. Sometimes if I wander round a dog cemetery, the words on the tombs, like the Victorian epitaph 'Born a dog: died a gentleman', raise a sad smile. More often, badly written as they are, the epitaphs make me weep. A sentiment in many of them, found also in a poem by Matthew Arnold, is that the individual dog – the unique personality – must be somehow celebrated and remembered.

I cannot read the verses that follow without tears coming to my eyes. Nor do I feel any shame about this. We owe our dogs the tribute of tears.

Just as love poetry preserves the memory of the mistress, so an epitaph to a dog holds back the darkness of oblivion. One of the best is this short verse by Robert Herrick. I am glad that in the title he preserved the name of his dog. This spaniel, who raced across the English countryside more than three hundred years ago, is thus rescued from forgetfulness.

## Upon My Spaniel, Tracie

Now thou art dead, no eye shall ever see
For shape and service spaniel like to thee.
This shall my love do, give thy sad death one
Tear, that deserves of me a million.

## Tribute to the Memory of a Dog, Music

Lie here, without a record of thy worth,
Beneath a covering of the common earth!
It is not from unwillingness to praise,
Or want of love, that here no stone we raise;
More thou deserv'st; but *this* man gives to man,
Brother to brother, *this* is all we can.
Yet they to whom thy virtues made thee dear
Shall find thee through all changes of the year:
This oak points out thy grave; the silent tree
Will gladly stand a monument to thee.

## In Sorrow and in Tears

We grieved for thee, and wished thy end were past;
And willingly have laid thee here at last:
For thou had yielded to the weight of years;
Extreme old age that wasted thee away,
And left thee but a glimmering of the day;
Thy ears were deaf, and feeble were thy knees, –
I saw thee stagger in the summer breeze,
Too weak to stand against its sportive breath,
And ready for the gentlest stroke of death.
It came, and we were glad; yet tears were shed;
Both man and woman wept when thou wert dead,
Not only for a thousand thoughts that were,
Old household thoughts, in which thou hadst thy share;
But for some precious boons vouchsafed to thee,
Found scarcely anywhere in like degree!

For love, that comes wherever life and sense
Are given by God, in thee was most intense;
A chain of heart, a feeling of the mind,
A tender sympathy, which did thee bind
Not only to us men, but to thy kind:
Yea, for thy fellow-brutes in thee we saw
A soul of love, love's intellectual law: –
Our tears from passion and from reason came,
And, therefore, shalt thou be an honoured name.

WILLIAM WORDSWORTH

Some epitaphs convey a really good idea of the dogs concerned. Sydney Smith's verses about a dog called Nick make me feel I know him. I can see him trotting courteously and contentedly down the street at Cheam. A lovely poem.

## Exemplary Nick

Here lies poor Nick, an honest creature,
Of faithful, gentle, courteous nature;
A parlour pet unspoiled by favour,
A pattern of good dog behaviour.
Without a wish, without a dream,
Beyond his home and friends at Cheam,
Contentedly through life he trotted
Along the path that fate allotted;
Till Time, his aged body wearing,
Bereaved him of his sight and hearing,
Then laid him down without a pain
To sleep, and never wake again.

The Scottish poet Robert Burns wrote several epitaphs for dogs. His poem about the death of a sheepdog is perhaps the most touching.

## My Hoggie

What will I do gin my Hoggie
    die?
My joy, my pride, my Hoggie!
My only beast, I had nae mae,
And vow but I was vogie!
The lee-lang night we watch'd
    the fauld,
Me and my faithfu' doggie;
We heard nocht but the roaring
    linn,
Amang the braes sae scroggie.

But the howlet cry'd frae the
    castle wa',
The blitter frae the boggie;
The tod reply'd upon the hill,
I trembled for my Hoggie.
When day did daw and cocks
    did craw,
The morning it was foggie;
An unco tyke lap o'er the dyke,
And maist has kill'd my Hoggie!

ROBERT BURNS

## Geist's Grave

Four years! – and didst thou stay above
The ground which hides thee now but four?
And all that life, and all that love,
Were crowded, Geist! into no more?

That loving heart, that patient soul,
Had they indeed no longer span,
To run their course, and reach their goal,
And read their homily to man?

That liquid, melancholy eye,
From whose pathetic, soul-fed springs
Seemed surging the Virgilian cry,
The sense of tears in mortal things–

That steadfast, mournful strain, consoled
By spirits gloriously gay,
And temper of heroic mould –
What, was four years their whole short day?

Yes, only four! – and not the course
Of all the centuries to come,
And not the infinite resource
Of Nature, with her countless sum

Of figures, with her fulness vast
Of new creation evermore,
Can ever quite repeat the past,
Or just thy little self restore.

But thou, when struck thine hour to go,
On us, who stood despondent by,
A meek last glance of love didst throw,
And humbly lay thee down to die.

Yet fondly zealous for thy fame,
Even to a date beyond thine own
We strive to carry down thy name,
By mounded turf and graven stone.

Then some, who through the garden pass,
When we too, like thyself are clay,
Shall see thy grave upon the grass,
And stop before the stone, and say –

'People who lived here long ago
Did by this stone, it seems, intend
To name for future times to know
The dachshund, Geist, their little friend.'

MATTHEW ARNOLD

[75]

I must find space for two more short epitaphs, neither by great poets. But both of them have something special for me. Perhaps the William Watson epitaph is sentimental. I do not care. I find it full of feeling.

## Epitaph on a Favourite Dog

Not hopeless, round this calm sepulchral spot,
A wreath, presaging life, we twine;
If God be love, what sleeps below was not
Without a spark divine.

SIR FRANCIS HASTINGS DOYLE

## An Epitaph

His friends he loved. His fellest earthly foes –
Cats – I believe he did but feign to hate.
My hand will miss the insinuated nose,
Mine eyes the tail that wagged contempt at fate.

WILLIAM WATSON

## A Popular Personage at Home

'I live here: Wessex is my name;
I am a dog known rather well:
I guard the house; but how that came
To be my whim I cannot tell.

'With a leap and a heart elate I go
At the end of an hour's expectancy
To take a walk of a mile or so
With the folk I let live here with me.

'Along the path, amid the grass
I sniff, and find out rarest smells
For rolling over as I pass
The open fields towards the dells.

'No doubt I shall always cross this sill,
And turn the corner, and stand steady,
Gazing back for my mistress till
She reaches where I have run already,

'And that this meadow with its brook,
And bulrush, even as it appears
As I plunge by with hasty look
Will stay the same a thousand years.'

Thus Wessex. But a dubious ray
At times informs his steadfast eye,
Just for a trice, as though to say,
'Yet, will this pass, and pass shall I?'

THOMAS HARDY

[77]

In the garden of Newstead Abbey, his family home, Byron built a monument to Boatswain, his Newfoundland dog. First came an inscription, then some verses. Both are justly famous.

Near this spot
Are deposited the Remains
of one
Who possessed Beauty
Without Vanity,
Strength without Insolence,
Courage without Ferocity,
And all the Virtues of Man
Without his Vices.

This Praise, which would be unmeaning flattery
If inscribed over Human Ashes,
Is but a just tribute to the Memory of
'Boatswain', a Dog
Who was born at Newfoundland
May, 1803,
And died at Newstead Abbey
Nov. 18, 1808.

## To Boatswain

When some proud son of man returns to earth,
Unknown to glory, but upheld by birth,
The sculptor's art exhausts the pomp of woe,
And storied urns record who rests below;
When all is done, upon the tombs is seen,
Not what he was, but what he should have been:
But the poor dog, in life the firmest friend,
The first to welcome, foremost to defend,
Whose honest heart is still his master's own,
Who labours, fights, lives, breathes for him alone,
Unhonoured falls, unnoticed all his worth,
Denied in heaven the soul he held on earth;
While man, vain insect! hopes to be forgiven,
And claims himself a sole, exclusive heaven.
O man! thou feeble tenant of an hour,
Debased by slavery, or corrupt by power,
Who knows thee well must quit thee with disgust,
Degraded mass of animated dust!
Thy love is lust, thy friendship all a cheat,
Thy smiles hypocrisy, thy words deceit!
By nature vile, ennobled but by name,
Each kindred brute might bid thee blush for shame.
Ye! who, perchance, behold this simple urn,
Pass on – it honours none you wish to mourn:
To mark a friend's remains these stones arise:
I never knew but one, and here he lies.

Apoem by Rudyard Kipling sums up the pain of sharing your life with a dog. I do not like all Kipling's dog poems. For he often writes in baby talk, as if all dogs were children. While I acknowledge that dogs keep the playfulness of the child (just as some lucky humans do), they are also serious, adult and grave in their loving. But this poem avoids excessive sentimentality.

## The Power of the Dog

There is sorrow enough in the natural way
From men and women to fill our day;
But when we are certain of sorrow in store,
Why do we always arrange for more?
*Brothers and sisters, I bid you beware
Of giving your heart to a dog to tear.*

Buy a puppy and your money will buy
Love unflinching that cannot lie –
Perfect passion and worship fed
By a kick in the ribs or a pat on the head.
*Nevertheless it is hardly fair
To risk your heart for a dog to tear.*

When the fourteen years which Nature permits
Are closing in asthma, or tumour, or fits,
And the vet's unspoken prescription runs
To lethal chambers or loaded guns,
*Then you will find – it's your own affair,*
*But… you've given your heart to a dog to tear.*

When the body that lived at your single will,
When the whimper of welcome is stilled (how still),
When the spirit that answered your every mood
Is gone – wherever it goes – for good,
*You will discover how much you care,*
*And will give your heart to a dog to tear!*

We've sorrow enough in the natural way,
When it comes to burying Christian clay.
Our loves are not given, but only lent,
At compound interest of cent. per cent.
Though it is not always the case, I believe,
That the longer we've kept 'em, the more do we grieve:
For when debts are payable, right or wrong,
A short-time loan is as bad as a long.
*So why in Heaven (before we are there!)*
*Should we give our hearts to a dog to tear?*

# IN HOPE OF DOGS IN HEAVEN

For those who have loved and lost a dog, there is sadness upon sadness. When one of our human family dies, we can often comfort ourselves with the thought that there may be an afterlife, that perhaps the individual is not simply deleted leaving no trace behind him.

But what of our dogs? I cannot imagine a heaven would be heaven without the familiar animals that have given me so much love. I feel like Anna Hempstead Branch who wrote:

> 'If there is no God for thee,
> Then there is no God for me.'

Like so many others before me, I have no doubt that the dogs I have known well, though intellectually inferior, have usually been my moral superior. They have, all of them, loved with an unconditional joy and simplicity that I can never achieve.

There is another quality that makes all animals holier than most of us men and women. 'The bliss of the animals lies in this, that, on their lower level,' wrote the novelist and minister George Macdonald, 'they shadow the bliss of those – few at any moment on the earth – who do not "look before and after, and pine for what is not" but live in the holy carelessness of the eternal now.'

I cannot bear to believe that the Christian promise of a life after death will be offered only to humans. But there is hope. 'We know that the whole creation groaneth and travaileth in pain together until now,' wrote St Paul, suggesting that Christ will come for all creation, not just the single human species, while St John the Divine foresaw a heaven in which 'every creature which is in heaven and on the earth' was blessing the lamb upon the throne.

Others have felt like I do, as several of the following poems and writings show. George Eliot declared: 'Shall we, because we walk on our hind feet, assume to ourselves only the privilege of imperishability? Shall we, who are even as they though we wag our tongues and not our tails, demand a special Providence and a selfish salvation?'

Then there is the conversation reported by the poet Robert Southey. Sir John Danvers was asked what had happened to his dog. 'Gone to heaven,' he replied. 'Then, Sir John,' said his friend, 'I hope now that you will follow him, for he has often followed you.' Finally there are the loving words of the great founder of the Protestant church, Martin Luther: 'Be comforted, little dog, thou too in the Resurrection, shall have a little golden tail.'

## His Dog is Dead

Oh friend of man! Blest being! You that shared
Your master's hunger and his meals as well!
You that in days of old in pilgrimage fared
With young Tobias and the angel Rafael.

Servant that loved me with a love intense,
As saints love God, my great exemplar be!
The mystery of your strange intelligence
Dwells in a guiltless, glad eternity.

*Dear Lord! If You should grant me by Your grace*
*To see You face to face in heaven, O then*
*Grant that a poor dog look into the face*
*Of him who was his god here among men!*

FRANCIS JAMMES

Robert Southey, a friend of Wordsworth and Coleridge, wrote this poem about the death of his own spaniel. He was twenty-two years old at the time and the dog had been his childhood companion.

## On the Death of a
## Favourite Old Spaniel

And they have drowned thee then at last, poor Phillis!
The burden of old age was heavy on thee,
And yet thou shouldst have lived! What though thine eye
Was dim, and watched no more with eager joy
The wonted call that on thy dull sense sunk
With fruitless repetition, the warm sun
Might still have cheered thy slumbers; thou didst love
To lick the hand that fed thee, and though past
Youth's active season, even life itself
Was comfort. Poor old friend, how earnestly
Would I have pleaded for thee! thou hadst been
Still the companion of my boyish sports:
And as I roamed o'er Avon's woody cliffs,
From many a daydream has thy short quick bark
Recalled my wandering soul. I have beguiled
Often the melancholy hours at school,
Soured by some little tyrant, with the thought
Of distant home, and I remembered then
Thy faithful fondness; for not mean the joy,
Returning at the pleasant holidays,
I felt from thy dumb welcome. Pensively
Sometimes have I remarked thy slow decay,
Feeling myself changed too, and musing much
On many a sad vicissitude of life!

Ah poor companion! When thou followedst last
Thy master's footsteps to the gate
Which closed for ever on him, thou didst lose
Thy truest friend and none was left to plead
For the old age of brute fidelity.
But fare thee well! Mine is no narrow creed;
And He who gave thee being did not frame
The mysteries of life to be the sport
Of merciless man! There is another world
For all that live and move – a better one!
Where the proud bipeds who would fain confine
Infinite goodness to the little bounds
Of their own charity, may envy thee!

The poet Alexander Pope believed that the intellectual gulf between man and dog was not impassable. 'Man has reason enough only to know what is necessary for him to know, and dogs have just that too,' he maintained. Somebody said to him: 'But then they must have souls too.' Pope replied: 'And what harm would that be to us?' These beautiful lines of his come from his poem, *An Essay on Man*.

Hope humbly then; with trembling pinions soar;
Wait the great teacher, death; and God adore!
What future bliss, he gives not thee to know,
But gives that hope to be thy blessing now,
Hope springs eternal in the human breast;
Man never is, but always to be blest:
The soul uneasy, and confined at home,
Rests, and expatiates in a life to come.
Lo! the poor Indian, whose untutored mind
Sees God in clouds, or hears him in the wind;
His soul, proud science never taught to stray
Far as the solar walk, or milky way;
Yet simple nature to his hope has given,
Behind the cloud-topped hill, an humbler heaven;
Some safer world in depth of woods embraced,
Some happier island in the wat'ry waste,
Where slaves once more their native land behold,
No fiends torment, no Christians thirst for gold.
To be, contents his natural desire,
He asks no angel's wing, no seraph's fire;
But thinks, admitted to that equal sky,
His faithful dog shall bear him company.

Pope's poem in turn inspired Horace Walpole, who like so many of us, could not bear to think of being parted for ever from his little dog, Rosette. During her last illness he wrote to his friend the Countess of Ossory: 'My poor Rosette is dying. She relapsed into her fits the last night of my stay at Nuneham, and has suffered exquisitely ever since. You may believe I have too; I have been out of bed twenty times every night, have had no sleep, and sat up with her till three this morning.' Thanks to his devoted care, the little dog lived on three more months. When she finally died, he wrote this.

*To Lord Nuneham, Saturday 6 November 1773*
'The rest of my time has been employed in nursing Rosette – alas! to no purpose. After suffering dreadfully for a fortnight from the time she was seized at Nuneham, she has only languished till about ten days ago. As I have nothing to fill my letter, I will send you her epitaph – it has no merit, for it is an imitation, but in coming from the heart…

Sweetest roses of the year
Strew around my Rose's bier.
Calmly may the dust repose
Of my pretty faithful Rose!
And if yon cloud-topped hill behind,
This frame dissolved, this breath resigned,
Some happier Isle, some humbler Heaven
Be to my trembling wishes given,
Admitted to that equal sky
May sweet Rose bear me company.

The French romantic poet Alphonse de Lamartine has written some of the most moving lines about dogs. When he wrote the verses, it was fashionable in scientific circles to argue that dogs and other animals were just 'living machines', without intelligence and without even feelings. Lamartine's poem is an impassioned argument against a theory that, alas, caused immense cruelty.

## O Dog of Mine

O dog of mine! Only God can measure
The distance between us on the scale of life
Between your instinct and your master's soul;
He only understands that strange affinity
By which you see through your master's eyes and even die
His death; He knows too that pity for the broken-hearted
- His gift to you, who go on loving
Those that no one else can love.
Never, poor beast that lies there on the ground,
Has my foot spurned you with ignorant disdain;
Never with brutal word embittering your
   love
Has my heart turned from your caressing
   touch.
But always and ever in you I have
   honoured
The boundless goodness of your Lord
   and mine, –
Just as we honour those the least of all
His creatures, brothers with a closeness
   Nature wills.

Ah, poor my Fido, when your eyes meet mine,
Silence can understand our wordless speech;
When, as you lie beside my bed gazing to see
If I am still alive, and when a single changing breath
Wakes you; when, reading sadness in my darkened
    eyes
You search my forehead for those lines of care,
And gently take between your teeth my offered
    hand
To chase away my melancholy thoughts;
When like a clear mirror, my sorrow or my joy
Bring to your loving eyes anxiety or calm,
So that the soul in you is clearly seen
And your love quite surpasses mere intelligence;
No, you are more than an illusion of a soul,
More than a mocking imitation of humanity,
More than a body responding to my touch,
More than a mere machine of life and love.

No, when the love that lights up in your eyes goes out,
It will come back to life somehow, somewhere in heaven.
That man or beast, who loves with such a tender sympathy,
Can never die or be extinct for ever.
God shatters for a moment, only to make whole.
For His embrace is wide enough to hold us all
And we will love each other as we loved in life.
What matters souls or instincts in His sight?
Wherever friendship consecrates a loving heart,
Wherever Nature lights the flame of love,
There God will not snuff out his divine spark
Not in the splendour of a night star's blaze
Nor in a humble spaniel's loving gaze.

Algernon Charles Swinburne, the Victorian poet, wrote a lovely poem about a dog's grave. After a rackety life drinking too much, he went to live in Putney where he used to wander about looking at babies in prams.

## At a Dog's Grave

Good night, we say, when comes the time to win
The daily death divine that shuts up sight,
Sleep, that assures for all who dwell therein
     Good night.

The shadow shed round those we love shines bright
As love's own face, when death, sleep's gentler twin,
From them divides us even as night from light.

Shall friends born lower in life, though pure of sin,
Though clothed with love and faith to usward plight,
Perish and pass unbidden of us, their kin,
     Good night?

To die a dog's death once was held for shame.
Not all men so beloved and mourned shall lie
As many of these, whose time untimely came
     To die.

His years were full: his years were joyous: why
Must love be sorrow, when his gracious name
Recalls his lovely life of limb and eye?

If aught of blameless life on earth may claim
Life higher than death, though death's dark wave rise high,
Such life as this among us never came
          To die.

White violets, there by hands more sweet than they
Planted, shall sweeten April's flowerful air
About a grave that shows to night and day
          White violets there.

A child's light hands, whose touch makes flowers more fair,
Keep fair as these for many a March and May
The light of days that are because they were.

It shall not like a blossom pass away;
It broods and brightens with the days that bear
Fresh fruits of love, but leave, as love might pray,
          White violets there.

I leave the last words to John Galsworthy, the playwright and novelist. He and his wife Ada believed that his dead spaniel, Chris, once came back to visit his owners. They also acknowledged that the best memorial for a dog is not found in books. It is written on the heart.

How many thousand walks did we not go together, so that we still turn to see if he is following at his padding gait, attentive to the invisible trails. Not the least hard thing to bear when they go from us, these quiet friends, is that they carry away with them so many years of our own lives. Yet, if they find warmth therein, who would grudge them those years that they have so guarded? Nothing else of us can they take to lie upon with outstretched paws and chin pressed to the ground; and, whatever they take, be sure they have deserved.

Do they know, as we do, that their time must come? Yes, they know, at rare moments. No other way can I interpret those pauses of his latter life, when, propped on his forefeet, he would sit for long minutes quite motionless – his head drooped, utterly withdrawn; then turn those eyes of his and look at me. That look said more plainly than all words could: 'Yes, I know that I must go!' If *we* have spirits that persist – *they* have. If *we* know after our departure who we were – *they* do. No one, I think, who really longs for truth, can ever glibly say which it will be for dog and man – persistence or extinction of our consciousness. There is but one thing certain – the childishness of fretting over that eternal question. Whichever it be, it must be right, the only possible thing. He felt that too, I know; but then, like his master, he was what is called a pessimist.

My companion tells me that, since he left us, he has once come back. It was Old Year's Night, and she was sad, when he came to her in visible shape of his black body, passing round the dining-room from the window-end, to his proper place beneath the table at her feet. She saw him quite clearly; she heard the padding tap-tap of his paws and very toe-nails; she felt his warmth brushing hard against the front of her skirt. She thought then that he would settle down upon her feet, but something disturbed him, and he stood pausing, pressed against her, then moved out toward where I generally sit, but was not sitting that night. She saw him stand there, as if considering; then at some sound or laugh, she became self-conscious, and slowly, very slowly, he was no longer there. Had he some message, some counsel to give, something he would say, that last night of the last year of all those he had watched over us? Will he come back again?

No stone stands over where he lies. It is on our hearts that his life is engraved.

# Acknowledgements

For permission to reproduce copyright material in this book, the author and publisher gratefully acknowledge the following:

*Pugolatry* by Haro Hodson, copyright © Haro Hodson; O *Pug* by Stevie Smith, copyright © Stevie Smith. Reprinted by permission of New Directions Publishing Corporation and James MacGibbon; extract from *My Rover* by John Clare, copyright © Curtis Brown & John Farquharson, 162–168 Regent Street, London W1R 5TB; *The Letters of Elizabeth Barrett Browning to Mary Russell Mitford*, edited by Meredith B Raymond and Mary Rose Sullivan (Wedgestone Press, 1983). Used by arrangement with John Murray (Publishers) Ltd; quotation from Konrad Lorenz, copyright © Methuen & Co Ltd, 11 New Fetter Lane, London EC4P 4EE; extract from *The Book of the Superiority of Dogs Over Those Who Wear Clothes* by Ibn al-Marzuban, copyright © Aris & Phillips Ltd, Teddington House, Warminster, Wiltshire BA12 8PQ; James McAcree for the translation of *O Dog of Mine* by Alphonse de Lamartine.

Picture credits

*By the Day's Bag* by Arthur Wardle, Bonhams; *Miss Jane Bowles* by Joshua Reynolds, The Wallace Collection, Manchester Square, London W1M 6BN; *The Shepherd's Chief Mourner* by Edwin Landseer, Victoria & Albert Museum, London SW7 2RL; *None for Me* by Edward John Cobbett, Fine Art Photos; *Two English Setters* by Arthur Wardle; *Portrait of a Golden Retriever* by Lilian Cheviot, Sara Davenport Gallery, 206 Walton Street, London SW3 2JL; *A Scottish and a Sealyham Terrier* by Lilian Cheviot, Fine Art Photos. W & F C Bonhams, Auctioneers, Montpelier Street, London SW7 1HH, hold regular sales of dog pictures.

Whilst every attempt has been made to trace the copyright holders, this has not always been possible. Any omissions will be rectified in future reprints.